Noah Webster's

Advice to the Young

and Moral Catechism

Foreword by
David Barton

Aledo, Texas

Noah Webster's Advice to the Young and Moral Catechism
Copyright © 1993, David Barton
4th Edition, 3rd Printing, 2012

Additional materials available from:
WallBuilders
P. O. Box 397
Aledo, TX 76008
(817) 441-6044
www.wallbuilders.com

Cover Illustration:
Gary Overacre
3802 Vineyard Trace
Marietta, GA 30062

Cover Design:
Jeremiah Pent
Lincoln-Jackson
838 Walden Dr.
Franklin, TN 37064

Barton, David
Noah Webster's Advice to the Young and Moral Catechism.
Aledo, TX: WallBuilder Press
53 p.; 21.5 cm.

ISBN 10: 0-925279-34-X
ISBN 13: 978-0-925279-34-7

Printed in the United States of America

Noah Webster

Noah Webster is a name recognized by most Americans today, primarily because of the dictionary which bears his name. His achievements, however, go well beyond that momentous work. In fact, for his other extensive efforts in early American education, he has been titled "America's Schoolmaster." Actually, however, it was his early activities related to the emergence of America as an independent, self-governing nation which first caused him to focus on education.

Additionally, Noah Webster was one of America's Founding Fathers, first helping her become independent during the American Revolution, and then helping establish her under a federal Constitution. He realized – like most of the other Founding Fathers – that for America to survive as an independent, self-governing nation, it would need much more than just a new form of government. As explained by Benjamin Rush, a signer of the Declaration of Independence and a leading educator:

> We have changed our forms of government, but it remains yet to effect a revolution in our principles, opinions, and manners so as to accommodate them to the forms of government we have adopted. This is the most difficult part of the business of the patriots and legislators of our country. . . . [E]ducation alone will render the American Revolution a blessing to mankind. [1]

The Founders realized that the quality of our new government would depend upon the quality of our education. In fact, education became so important to our Founders that in the ten years following the American Revolution, more colleges and universities were established in America than in the 150 years preceding the Revolution. [2]

The Founders' involvement in education was diverse: some authored textbooks (e.g., Benjamin Rush, Jedediah Morse); some worked on educational policies and legislation (e.g., George Washington and Rufus King); and some founded universities (e.g., Benjamin Franklin and the University of Pennsylvania, Thomas Jefferson and the University of Virginia, Abraham Baldwin and the University of Georgia). Noah Webster was one of the few Founding Fathers who participated in all of these aspects of education.

---

1. Benjamin Rush, *Letters of Benjamin Rush*, L. H. Butterfield, editor (Princeton: The American Philosophical Society, published by Princeton University Press, 1951), Vol. I, pp. 388-389, to Richard Price on May 25, 1786.

2. Benjamin Rush, *A Letter by Dr. Benjamin Rush Describing the Consecration of the German College at Lancaster* (Lancaster, PA: Franklin and Marshall College, 1945), pp. 9-10.

Born in Hartford, Connecticut, in 1758, Noah came from a family with a history of leadership. His mother was a descendant of Governor William Bradford of the Pilgrims, and his father was a descendant of John Webster, an early governor of Connecticut.

Noah spent his childhood years learning the discipline of farm life on his family's small farm. In 1774, his father mortgaged the farm to raise the money to send Noah to Yale, where his studies were interrupted several times by the Revolution. In fact, Noah twice left Yale to join the fighting, once marching to Canada in 1776, and then marching with his father's company of militia to the field of battle at Saratoga to participate in the surrender of British General Burgoyne in 1777.

Noah finally graduated from Yale in 1778 amid a class of many others who distinguished themselves. This class included Joel Barlow (chaplain in the American Revolution and foreign counsel for President George Washington), Uriah Tracy (a Major-General, US Representative, and US Senator), Oliver Wolcott, Jr. (a son of the signer of the Declaration of Independence, successor of Alexander Hamilton as Secretary of State under President George Washington, and later Governor of Connecticut), and many other luminaries.

Upon Noah's graduation, his father gave him eight dollars in Continental currency and told him that henceforth he must support himself. Noah returned to Hartford and began teaching school while pursuing the study of law. After three years, in 1781 he was admitted to the bar; and during part of his studies, he lived in the home of attorney Oliver Ellsworth, [3] who later became a delegate to the Constitutional Convention and then a Chief Justice of the US Supreme Court.

Noah's three years of teaching school first revealed to him the weaknesses of American education: it was too reliant on the British. Not only did many young Americans travel overseas to study in British and other foreign colleges, but American schools used British geography and literature books and even taught British meanings for words. Webster explained the weaknesses of this system:

> [T]he institutions in this country which are new and peculiar give rise to new terms or to new applications of old terms. . . . Thus the terms *land-office; land-warrant; location of land; consociation* of churches; *regent* of a university; *intendant* of a city; . . . &c., are either

---

3. Noah Webster, *An American Dictionary of the English Language* (Springfield: George and Charles Merriam, 1849), "Memoir of the Author," p. xv.

words not belonging to the language of England, or they are applied to things in this country which do not exist in that. No person in this country will be satisfied with the English definitions of the words *congress, senate, assembly, court,* &c. . . . But this is not all. . . . [T]he English dictionaries inform us that a *justice* is one deputed by the *king* to do right by way of judgment – he is a *lord* by his office – justices of the peace are appointed by the *king's commission* – language which is inaccurate in respect to this officer in the United States. . . . [and which] requires a different definition. [4]

Webster understood that a continued attachment to Great Britain in education might lead to a return to her politics; he realized that there was a clear connection between popular education and popular sovereignty. Recognizing that – as he told one friend – "America must be as independent in literature as she is in politics," [5] he therefore began to promote a distinctly American system of education.

In 1785, he embarked on a speaking tour across the nation to promote American education. His lectures from this tour were later published as *Dissertations on the English Language,* and in those lectures he announced to the nation:

Now is the time . . . in which we may expect success in attempting changes favorable to language, science and government. . . . Let us then seize the present moment and establish a national language as well as a national government. [6]

Webster had long believed that an integral part of a new American system of education was new, purely American textbooks. In fact, as he had once explained, even before the end of the American Revolution he had begun to write such textbooks:

In the year 1782, while the American army was lying on the bank of the Hudson, I kept a classical school [The Farmer's Hall Academy] in Goshen, Orange County, State of New York. I there compiled two small elementary books for teaching the English language. [7]

---

4. Webster's *Dictionary* (1849), "Author's Preface," p. xii.

5. Noah Webster, *The Letters of Noah Webster,* Harry R. Warfel, editor (New York: Library Press, 1953), p. 4, to John Canfield on January 6, 1783.

6. Noah Webster, *Dissertations on the English Language* (Boston: Isaiah Thomas and Company, 1789), p. 406, "An Essay on the Necessity, Advantages, and Practicability of Reforming the Mode of Spelling, and of Rendering the Orthography of Words Correspondent to the Pronunciation."

7. Horace Scudder, *Noah Webster* (Boston: Houghton, Mifflin, & Co., 1889), p. 33.

By the time Webster published those books, the "two small elementary books" had expanded to three, entitled *Grammatical Institutes of the English Language.* The first volume (1783) was an American speller and introduced the Americanized spelling of British words (e.g., "labor," "honor," and "public" instead of "labour," "honour," and "publick"). Benjamin Franklin (who had long advocated spelling reforms) had a significant influence on Webster's philosophy of spelling. As Webster later explained to George Washington:

> I am encouraged . . . to proceed in my design of refining the language and improving our general system of education. Dr. Franklin has extended my views to a very simple plan of reducing the language to perfect regularity. [8]

(Incidentally, the "moral catechism" we have reprinted in this booklet was taken from Webster's *Speller.*)

The second volume of Webster's trio was an American grammar book (1784), and the third volume was an American reader (1785). These new texts were praised by many of America's greatest statesmen, including George Washington, [9] Timothy Pickering, [10] Benjamin Franklin, [11] and others.

In 1787, Webster revised the reader (the third volume of his *Institutes*), and into the title of this edition Webster first inserted the word "American." As he told Benjamin Franklin, this new American reader contained:

> . . . some *American* pieces upon the discovery, history, wars, geography, economy, commerce, government, &c. of *this* country . . . in order to call the minds of our youth from ancient fables and modern foreign events and fix them upon objects immediately interesting in *this* country. [12] (emphasis added)

Webster's three volume *Institutes* were well received not only by America's leaders but also by her educators – evidenced by this early advertisement from the Thomas & Andrews edition:

---

8. Webster, *Letters*, p. 46, to George Washington on March 31, 1786.

9. George Washington, *The Writings of George Washington*, John C. Fitzpatrick, editor (Washington, DC: US Government Printing Office, 1988), Vol. 28, p. 216, to Noah Webster on July 30, 1785.

10. Timothy Pickering, *The Life of Timothy Pickering*, Octavius Pickering, editor (Boston: Little, Brown, and Company, 1867), Vol. I, pp. 529-531, in October 1785.

11. Benjamin Franklin, *The Works of Benjamin Franklin*, Jared Sparks, editor (Boston: Tappan, Whittemore, and Mason, 1840), Vol. X, pp. 412-413, to Noah Webster on December 26, 1789.

12. Webster, *Letters*, p. 44, to Benjamin Franklin in 1786.

The Introduction of Webster's *Institute* into all the Public Schools in the town of Boston, with the increasing demand for them in the country, added to the circumstance of its being the only complete system of school education ever published by an American author, has induced the subscribers to purchase the exclusive right of printing all the Three Parts of said *Institute* in the States of Massachusetts, Newhampshire, and Rhodeisland, for the term of fourteen years. [13]

While Webster's *Institutes* experienced national success, that success came at the cost of Webster's frustration of having to publish under thirteen autonomous state governments. Because there was no uniformity of laws between the states, Webster found little, no, or highly variable copyright protection for his works from state to state, and he thus had great difficulty in obtaining legal protections for those works.

This experience, coupled with his firm belief that students in each state should be taught the same common elements of an American education, caused him to align politically with the Federalists. In 1784-1785, Webster promoted his Federalist ideas and argued for a national system of government in his book *Sketches of American Policy*. This work was believed by many to be one of the first calls for a Constitution of the United States. [14]

While on his first national tour in 1785, Webster had visited Philadelphia where he consulted with leaders in Congress on his plan for an American system of education. Those leaders, including James Madison, had encouraged him in his pursuit. [15] In 1787, Webster returned to Philadelphia for a second visit and was there during the Constitutional Convention. (His visit turned into a stay of ten months when he became headmaster of an Episcopal academy.)

Having long advocated a new form of government, Webster closely watched the proceedings at the Convention. Many of the delegates not only knew of and respected Webster, but even dined with him or called on him at his home (e.g., George Washington, Edmund Randolph, Oliver Ellsworth, William Livingston, Roger Sherman, Jared Ingersoll, Ben Franklin, Abraham Baldwin, Timothy Pickering, and James Madison [16]).

---

13. Noah Webster, *An American Selection of Lessons in Reading and Speaking. . . . Being the Third Part of a Grammatical Institute of the English Language* (Boston: Isaiah Thomas and Ebenezer T. Andrews, 1799), p. iv.

14. Webster's *Dictionary* (1849), "Memoir," p. xvi.

15. Webster's *Dictionary* (1849), "Memoir," pp. xv-xvi.

16. Noah Webster, *The Autobiographies of Noah Webster*, Richard M. Rollins, editor (South Carolina: University of South Carolina Press, 1989), see diary entries from January through September, 1787.

Ideas born out of Webster's earlier frustrations with state copyright laws took root in the final product of that Convention. It was Webster's efforts – combined with those of Dr. David Ramsay (a member of the Continental Congress from South Carolina as well as an author, historian, and physician) which led to the inclusion of uniform copyright protection in Article 1, Section 8, ¶8 of the Constitution. (Ironically, considering Webster's efforts to obtain this copyright protection, his name eventually went into the public domain and was later attached to many works with which he had nothing whatever to do! [17])

Following the adjournment of the Constitutional Convention, members solicited Webster's assistance and asked him to exert his influence to help secure public acceptance of the new Constitution. [18] Webster responded enthusiastically and published *The Leading Principles of the Federal Constitution* (which he dedicated to Benjamin Franklin) to urge support and ratification of the new Federalist document.

While still in Philadelphia, Webster met Rebecca Greenleaf (the sister of a prominent businessman) and a courtship began. He then returned to New York where, in late 1787, he published the *American Magazine* to promote American education. In December of that same year, he returned to Hartford to practice law, and in October of the following year, Noah married Rebecca in Boston (her family home). They eventually became the parents of two sons (one of whom died in infancy) and six daughters.

In 1793, Webster moved from Hartford back to New York where he published a daily paper called the *Minerva* and a semi-weekly paper called the *Herald*. Both were strongly Federalist, and, as Webster explained, "were established for the purpose of vindicating and supporting the policy of President Washington." [19] (The two papers were later known as the *Commercial Advertiser* and the *New York Spectator*.)

In 1794, Webster shifted his attention from domestic affairs to the foreign scene. For example, France became a focus for his pen. In America, there was much concern over the French Revolution, for while many Americans supported the French effort for independence, they opposed the bloodbath and slaughter of innocent life which accompanied that revolution – a subject Webster addressed in *The Revolution in France*. Another international focus of his attention was Great Britain and the Jay Treaty. The Jay Treaty was negotiated by Founding Father John Jay to settle several difficulties between

---

17. *Webster's American Biographies*, s.v. "Webster, Noah."
18. Webster's *Dictionary* (1849), "Memoir," p. xvi.
19. Emily Ford, *Notes on the Life of Noah Webster* (New York, 1912), Vol. I, p. 386, n.

America and Great Britain which had arisen from violations of the treaty that had finalized the American Revolution. While the Jay Treaty was generally favorable for Americans (requiring the British to depart from their remaining posts in the northwest, giving America unrestricted navigation of the Mississippi, and guaranteeing equal privileges to American vessels in British ports), it also contained several provisions which angered many Americans (restricting American trade in the West Indies, not paying damages for Americans whose slaves had been carried off by Great Britain, and not protecting American seamen from British impressment). Despite these shortcomings, however, Webster believed that the treaty offered much, and in 1795, he published ten articles to urge support for it. Rufus King (signer of the Constitution and foreign Ambassador for Presidents George Washington, John Adams, Thomas Jefferson, and John Quincy Adams) directly credited Webster's articles with having caused the public acceptance of that treaty. [20]

In 1798, Webster again left New York, this time to return to New Haven, Connecticut, where he lived for the next fourteen years. During these years, he served several terms as a member of the Connecticut legislature, as a justice of the peace and as a member of the city council.

Despite his numerous political and civic activities, his educational efforts continued. Between 1802 and 1806, he published his *Elements of Useful Knowledge*, a three-volume work filled with American history, American geography, and several documents reflecting American government (e.g., the Constitution, and George Washington's "Farewell Address"). In 1806, he published his first dictionary, *A Compendious Dictionary of the American Language*. The following year, he published *A Philosophical and Practical Grammar of the English Language* and also began work on his great dictionary – a herculean effort that consumed much of his attention over the next two decades.

(Although this brief overview of Webster's life has emphasized his frequent written excursions into politics and basic education, Webster's expertise and abilities were much broader. For example, in 1799, he published "On the Supposed Change in the Temperature of Winter" which foreshadowed the work of the census and weather bureaus of later times. [21] In 1800, he authored a two-volume medical work, *A Brief History of Epidemic and Pestilential Diseases*, which was used as a textbook in medical schools, [22] being described as the most important medical work written

---

20. *Appletons' Cyclopaedia of American Biography*, s.v. "Webster, Noah."

21. *Dictionary of American Biography*, s.v. "Webster, Noah."

22. Rush, *Letters*, Vol. II, pp. 811-812 and 828, letters to Noah Webster on June 20, 1799, and December 9, 1800.

by a layman. [23] And in 1836, he penned an economic work entitled "The Origin and State of Banking Institutions and Insurance Offices" which examined the rights of neutrals and the right of blockades.)

In 1812, Webster moved to Amherst, Massachusetts, where he continued working on his dictionary and helped found Amherst College, becoming its first president of the board of trustees. While in Massachusetts, Webster served three terms in the state legislature, working to secure permanent funding for an educational system that would "discipline our youth in early life in sound maxims of moral, political, and religious duties." [24] In 1822, he returned to New Haven where Yale awarded him a Doctorate of Civil Law.

In 1824, still working on his massive dictionary, Webster traveled to England and France to examine literary works not available in America and to consult with other experts on word usage. There, he made a final collection of useful and necessary materials and completed his manuscript before returning to America. (Incidentally, in preparing the dictionary and seeking to understand the origin and etymology of words, Webster learned over twenty languages! [25])

In 1828, his two-volume masterpiece was published: *A Dictionary of the English Language.* That dictionary – containing 12,000 words and 40,000 definitions not found in any previous dictionary – was the first to record nonliterary words and to include American meanings and "Americanisms." His work was described as "the most ambitious publication ever undertaken up to that time upon American soil." [26]

During the twenty years that Webster had dedicated himself to the compilation and writing of his comprehensive dictionary, he supported himself and his family from the income received from the sales of his *Institutes.* Although the royalty from each sale was small (less than one-cent per copy), the volume had been enormous: nearly a million copies a year! [27] By his death in 1843, some 404 editions had appeared; by 1847, twenty-four million copies had been purchased by schools and the public; [28] and by 1889,

---

23. *A Bibliography of the Writings of Noah Webster,* Edwin H. Carpenter, Jr., editor (New York: Arno Press, Inc., 1971), p. 347, quoting Sir William Osler, "Some Aspects of Medical Bibliography," *Bulletin* of the Association of Medical Librarians, July-October, 1902, Vol. I, p. 27.

24. Ford, *Notes,* Vol. II, pp. 156-157, to Solomon Snead on March 30, 1820.

25. Webster's *Dictionary* (1849), "Author's Preface," p. xi. See also Harry R. Warfel, *Noah Webster: Schoolmaster to America* (New York: The Macmillan Company, 1936), p. 348.

26. *Dictionary of American Biography,* s.v. "Webster, Noah."

27. Noah Webster, *The Elementary Spelling Book* (New York: G. F. Cooledge & Brother, 1848), advertisement in front of speller.

28. Webster's *Dictionary* (1849), "Memoir," p. xvi.

the number had increased to sixty-two million! [29] (Eventually, over one hundred million copies of his *Speller* sold; in 1936, it was still in use in schools; and as late as 1975, two editions still appeared in print. [30])

In 1832, Webster revised his three-volume *Elements of Useful Knowledge* into a single, small history book for schools called *The History of the United States*. It was clearly an American view of history; and just as his *Institutes* helped shape the structure of American language, this work helped shape the teaching of American history. In fact, one education group claimed: "The obligation of our common schools to Noah Webster for his early work in promoting the study of our history is incalculable." [31]

Webster's "Advice to the Young," which we have reprinted in this booklet, is taken from *The History of the United States*. Of this, Webster explained:

> The "Advice to the Young," it is hoped, will be useful in enlightening the minds of youth in religious and moral principles, and serve, in a degree, to restrain some of the common vices of our country. Republican government loses half of its value where the moral and social duties are imperfectly understood or negligently practiced. To exterminate our popular vices is a work of far more importance to the character and happiness of our citizens than any other improvements in our system of education. [32]

In addition to the books already mentioned, Webster authored numerous others, including *The Little Reader's Assistant* (1790), *The Prompter* (1791), *The Peculiar Doctrines of the Gospel Explained and Defended* (1809), *The History of Animals* (1812), *Letters to a Young Man Commencing His Education* (1823), *A Revision of the Authorized Version of the English Bible* (1833), *The Value of the Bible* (1834), *Observations on Language* (1839), *A Collection of Papers on Political, Literary, and Moral Subjects* (1843), and many other works. He also authored seemingly countless essays, pamphlets, and articles on a wide range of topics. [33]

---

29. *Appletons' Cyclopaedia of American Biography*, s.v. "Webster, Noah."

30. Richard M. Rollins, *The Long Journey of Noah Webster* (Pennsylvania: University of Pennsylvania Press, 1980), p. 35.

31. *Old South Leaflets* (Boston: Directors of the Old South Work, Old South Meeting House), Vol. VIII, p. 448.

32. Noah Webster, *History of the United States* (New Haven: Durrie and Peck, 1832), p. 6.

33. See *A Bibliography of the Writings of Noah Webster*, Edwin H. Carpenter, Jr., editor (New York: Arno Press, Inc., 1971).

Just as Webster's professional life displayed depth and profundity, so did his religious life – as explained by the memoir of his life which appeared in his comprehensive dictionary after his death. It explains that Webster once returned to Yale for a visit, unexpectedly finding himself in the midst of a campus revival. Impressed by what he saw, his memoir explained that he was inspired to . . .

> . . . inquire with an earnestness which he had never felt before into the nature of personal religion and the true ground of man's acceptance with God. He had now to decide not for himself only, but, to a certain extent, for others whose spiritual interests were committed to his charge. Under a sense of this responsibility, he took up the study of the Bible with painful solicitude. As he advanced, the objections which he had formerly entertained against the humbling doctrines of the Gospel were wholly removed. He felt their truth in his own experience. He felt that salvation must be wholly of grace. He felt constrained, as he afterward told a friend, to cast himself down before God, confess his sins, implore pardon through the merits of the Redeemer, and there to make his vows of entire obedience to the commands and to devotion to the service of his Maker. [34]

Webster desired to share this new-found influence in his life with his family. This was in no way surprising, though; for throughout his life, Webster had always demonstrated a strong attachment and total devotion to his family. (In fact, his wife Rebecca once wrote the children: "Papa longs to see you all. I heard someone conversing in the drawing room the other day and found him standing before your portraits." [35]) With such a love for his children, it was only natural that, having experienced the personal change brought into his life by Christianity and the Bible, he should carry it back to his family. His Memoir explained:

> [W]hile he had aimed at the faithful discharge of all his duties as their parent and head, he had neglected one of the most important: that of family prayer. After reading the Scriptures, he led them with deep solemnity to the throne of grace, and from that time continued the practice with the liveliest interest to the period of his death. [36]

Webster believed that instilling in his children a love and veneration for the Scriptures was the greatest legacy he could leave them. A confirmation

---

34. Webster's *Dictionary* (1849), "Memoir," p. xxii.
35. Warfel, *Schoolmaster*, p. 417.
36. Webster's *Dictionary* (1849), "Memoir," p. xxii.

of his commitment to this legacy was evidenced when thirty-five of his children, grandchildren, and great-grandchildren gathered in New Haven in 1842 to celebrate, three years late, the golden wedding anniversary of Noah and Rebecca. Noah's daughter, Eliza, described what transpired on that day:

> All the children, grandchildren, and great-grandchildren of the dear old patriarch [Noah] and his wife Rebecca were invited to gather. . . . Through the favor of a kind Providence, we came together in health and comfort at the appointed time, and sent a troop of happy little ones to escort the head of our house to the gathering table. Brother's parlor was filled. . . . There were only two present who could not sing, and all began in merry mood good "Auld Lang Syne" and then "Home Sweet Home" and tears of tenderness and joy followed. We dined at half past one. . . . When all were seated at the well filled board, brother G[oodrich] rose and fervently implored the blessing of heaven. We felt that God was with us and it was a cheerful meal. When we had finished, brother Fowler made a few remarks expressive of our gratitude to God that we had been permitted to meet such comfort, and that we were so united, loving and beloved, and returned solemn hearty thanks. Then we returned to the parlor to talk of old times and observe the happiness of the little folks whose eyes sparkled and whose smiles and laugh gladdened the hearts of us older folks who felt that we were to part never to meet all together again till we stand unsheltered before the Great Author of our being to learn where shall be our last eternal home. Twenty-one of us were professedly the children of grace, and the others – may they, too, come to the cross of Christ and find in Him their everlasting portion! At five we all went to Father's and took our tea in the home of our early days. In the evening before we parted, our beloved and revered parent called our attention, and kneeling, as we all did, fervently implored the blessing of heaven upon us, our children, and our children's children to the latest generation. Oh shall not that prayer be heard? Then rising, he said, it was the happiest day of his life, to see us all together; so many walking in the truth; and the others, children of promise. . . . Then he presented each of us with a Bible, his last gift, with our names written by his own trembling hand; and we closed our meeting by singing "Blest be the tie that binds." Shall we ever forget it? Oh no! The youngest there received some deep

impression of the blessedness of nurturing a family in the fear of God. Their little Bibles are cherished gifts. [37]

Noah Webster truly lived his life as a deeply committed Christian and obeyed the Scriptural injunction by bringing up his children "in the nurture and admonition of the Lord." [Ephesians 6:4]

Yet, for decades prior to this gathering, Noah Webster had been just as strongly committed to teaching those very same Biblical principles to all citizens and students. In fact, a fundamental tenet of his educational philosophy had been that Christian principles were inseparable from a successful educational system. As he explained:

> In my view, the Christian religion is the *most* important and one of the *first* things in which *all* children under a free government ought to be instructed. . . . No truth is more evident to my mind than that the Christian religion must be the basis of any government intended to secure the rights and privileges of a free people. [38] (emphasis added)

Notice, too, some of the advice to students from his textbooks:

> I would commend to you, at this early period of life, to become well acquainted with the Scriptures and with the facts and arguments which support their authenticity, and their divine original. Nothing is more common than for young men to fall into scepticism merely for want of a thorough knowledge of the Scriptures. [39]

> [I]t is the sincere desire of the writer that our citizens should early understand that the genuine source of correct republican principles is the Bible, particularly the New Testament or the Christian religion. [40]

> [T]he religion which has introduced civil liberty is the religion of Christ and His apostles, which enjoins humility, piety and benevolence; which acknowledges in every person a brother, or a sister, and a citizen with equal rights. This is genuine Christianity,

---

37. Ford, *Notes*, Vol. II, pp. 359-361, "An Account of the Festival of the Golden Wedding" by Eliza Webster Jones, May 1842.

38. Webster, *Letters*, p. 453, to David McClure on October 25, 1836.

39. Noah Webster, *Letters To A Young Gentleman Commencing His Education* (New Haven: Howe & Spalding, 1823), p. 63, Letter VI.

40. Webster, *History of the United States*, p. 6.

41. Webster, *History of the United States*, p. 300, ¶578.

and to this we owe our free constitutions of government. [41]

[T]he moral principles and precepts contained in the Scriptures ought to form the basis of all our civil constitutions and laws. . . . All the miseries and evils which men suffer from vice, crime, ambition, injustice, oppression, slavery, and war, proceed from their despising or neglecting the precepts contained in the Bible. [42]

And he reminded all citizens:

[S]in, even in this life, produces more pain and misery than real pleasure. No, my friend, there is no substantial satisfaction in this life, except in conforming to the laws of the Supreme Lawgiver. . . . [M]an enjoy[s] the most happiness when his heart is reconciled to the Divine laws and most conformed to the Divine character. . . . The soul of man is, I am persuaded, never tranquil till the will is subdued and has yielded with implicit submission to God's sovereign grace. [43]

Interestingly, so committed was Webster to the inculcation of these principles that even something as unlikely as his massive dictionary became a means for maintaining religious principles in national education. For example, Webster dedicated that great dictionary to God, explaining in its preface that:

To that great and benevolent Being, who during the preparation of this work, has sustained a feeble constitution [body] amidst obstacles and toils, disappointments, infirmities and depression; who has borne me and my manuscripts in safety across the Atlantic, and given me strength and resolution to bring the work to a close, I would present the tribute of my most grateful acknowledgments. And if the talent which He has entrusted to my care has not been put to the most profitable use in His service, I hope it has not been "kept laid up in a napkin" [Luke 19:20] and that any misapplication of it may be graciously forgiven. [44]

Additionally, after Webster defined each word, he would provide illustrations to clarify the meanings of the word; and a significant percentage of the thousands of examples he provided were Bible verses! But this was not surprising, for, as he had declared in the preface to that dictionary:

---

42. Webster, *History of the United States*, p. 339, ¶53.
43. Noah Webster, *The Peculiar Doctrines of the Gospel Explained and Defended* (New York: J. Seymour, 1809), pp. 9-10.
44. Webster's *Dictionary* (1849), "Author's Preface," p. xiv.

I present [this dictionary] to my fellow-citizens, not with frigid indifference, but with my ardent wishes for their improvement and happiness and . . . the moral and religious elevation of character, and the glory, of my country. [45]

Unfortunately, since its original publication in 1828, Webster's dictionary has undergone extensive censorship to remove its Christian nature; and although the most popular dictionary in America continues to bear his name, it no longer reflects the spirit of the original.

Noah Webster's life ended in 1843. Interestingly, citizens during those days often watched the death scene of a leader with great attention, for as one author explained:

[I]t is customary, even among Christian people, to withhold final judgment of a man's Christian character till it is seen how he makes his death. The manner of a man's death often works a change, sometimes a revolution, in public opinion respecting the nature of his life. [46]

So, did the manner in which Noah Webster die prove him to be less of a believer than the manner in which he lived? Just the contrary; his response to the final, terminal sickness which came upon him allowed him to display for the final time the strong Christian commitment which had characterized his long life. As reprinted in his Memoir, when the doctors reported to him that his illness was to be fatal . . .

He received the communication with surprise, but with entire composure. . . . He expressed his entire resignation to the will of God and his unshaken trust in the atoning blood of the Redeemer. . . . "I know in Whom I have believed" – such was the solemn and affecting testimony which he gave to his friend while the hand of death was upon him – "I know in Whom I have believed, and that He is able to keep that which I have committed unto Him against that day." Thus, without one doubt, one fear, he resigned his soul into the hands of his Maker, and died on the 28th day of May, 1843, in the eighty-fifth year of his age. [47]

45. Webster's *Dictionary* (1849), "Author's Preface," p. xiv.

46. B. F. Tefft, *[Daniel] Webster and His Master-Pieces* (Auburn: Miller, Orton, and Mulligan, 1854), p. 496.

47. Webster's *Dictionary* (1849), "Memoir," p. xxii.

Interestingly, this description of the life, character, and death of Noah Webster was included at the front of his great dictionary until the twentieth century! Can you imagine finding that account in the beginning of a *Webster Dictionary* today?

Noah Webster's lengthy and productive life proves him to be one of America's most brilliant and well-informed men; his profound influence on American education is irrefutable. In fact, only two years after his death, the publishers of his 1845 *Speller* summarized that influence:

> Webster, The Schoolmaster of our Republic. . . . has left us a standard of the English language which will guide all successive ages. . . . In this sense, Noah Webster is the all-shaping, all-controlling mind of this hemisphere. He grew up with his country and he molded the intellectual character of her people. Not a man has sprung from her soil on whom he has not laid his all-forming hand. His principles of language have tinged every sentence that is now, or will ever be uttered by an American tongue. . . . Only two men have stood on the New World whose fame is so sure to last – Columbus, its discoverer; and Washington, its savior. Webster is, and will be its great teacher; and these three make our trinity of fame. [48]

Since the school books written by Webster enjoyed widespread use for decades after his death, many of those texts featured a picture of Webster and a brief description of his life. Above his picture often appeared an epigraph which accurately described his life's work and goal:

Noah Webster taught millions to read, but not one to sin. [49]

---

48. William G. Webster, *A Speller and Definer* (Philadelphia: J. B. Lippincott Company, 1845), Foreword.

49. William G. Webster, *A Speller and Definer*, inside front cover.

HISTORY

OF THE

UNITED STATES;

TO WHICH IS PREFIXED

A BRIEF HISTORICAL ACCOUNT OF OUR

ENGLISH ANCESTORS,

FROM THE DISPERSION AT BABEL, TO THEIR MIGRA-
TION TO AMERICA ;

AND OF THE

CONQUEST OF SOUTH AMERICA,

BY THE SPANIARDS.

BY NOAH WEBSTER, LL. D.

NEW-HAVEN,
PUBLISHED BY DURRIE & PECK.

BALDWIN AND TREADWAY, PRINT

1832.

VIEW OF THE U.S. CAPITOL AT WASHINGTON.

ADVICE TO THE YOUNG.

1. My young friends, the first years of your life are to be employed in learning those things which are to make you good citizens, useful members of society, and candidates for a happy state in another world. Among the first things you are to learn are your duties to your parents. These duties are commanded by God, and are necessary to your happiness in this life. The commands of God are, " Honor thy father and thy mother."—" Children, obey your parents in all things." These commands are binding on all children; they cannot be neglected without sin. Whatever God has commanded us to do, we must perform, without calling in question the propriety of the command.

2. But the reasonableness of this command to obey parents is clear and easily understood by children, even when quite young. Parents are the natural guardians of their children. It is their duty to feed, clothe, protect and educate them; and for these purposes it is proper and necessary that parents should have authority to direct their actions. Parents therefore are bound by duty and by right to govern their children; but the exercise of this right is to be regulated by affection. Parents have implanted in them a tender love for their offspring,

which induces them to exercise authority over them with kindness.

3. It is proper that parents should be intrusted with the instruction of children, because children have every thing to learn, and parents are older and have gained a knowledge of what their children want to know. Parents have learned what is right, and what is wrong ; what is duty, and what is sin ; what is useful and what is hurtful to children and to men. And as children pass the first years of their life with their parents, they may be continually learning from their parents what is necessary or useful in the concerns of life.

4. It is not only proper that children should obey their parents, but their obedience should be prompt and cheerful. A slow, reluctant obedience, and that which is accompanied with murmurings, is not acceptable to parents nor to God. A sense of duty should make a child free and ready to comply with a parent's command ; and this will always be the case where the child entertains a due respect for his parents. Love and respect render obedience easy and cheerful, and a willing obedience increases the confidence of parents in their children, and strengthens their attachment to them. But a cold and unwilling obedience, with a murmuring disposition, alienates affection, and inclines the parent to rigor and severity in the exercise of his authority.

5. Hence it is a primary duty of children, and as much their interest as it is their duty to " Honor their father and their mother." This honor not only forbids the child to disobey his parents but it forbids all rudeness and ill manners towards them. Children should manifest their respect for their parents in all their actions. They should be modest and respectful in their company, never interrupting them in conversation, nor boldly contradicting them : they should address them as superiors, and yield to their opinions and admonitions. This subordination of chil-

dren to their parents is the foundation of peace in families; contributes to foster those kindly dispositions, both in parents and children, which are the sources of domestic happiness, and which extend their influence to all social relations in subsequent periods of life.

6. Among the first and most important truths which you are to learn, are those which relate to God and religion. As soon as your minds become capable of reasoning, or excited by curiosity to know the causes of things, you will naturally inquire who made the world, who made you, and why were you made? You will understand, by a moment's thought, that the things around you cannot have made themselves. You will be convinced that a stone or a mass of earth cannot have made itself, as it has no power in itself to act or move; it must then have had a creator, some being that had power to act or move, and to bring the stone into existence.

7. You observe that plants and trees grow, but they do not grow in winter, when it is cold; some degree of heat is necessary to their growth. You conclude then that wood and vegetable matter in itself has not the power of growth or increase. You see various animals, as dogs, and horses, but you know that they cannot create themselves; the first animal of every kind must then have had a creator, distinct from the animal himself. You see houses, and barns and ships, but you know that they did not make themselves; you know they are made by men. You know also that you did not create yourselves; you began to exist at a time which you cannot remember, and in a manner of which you have no knowledge.

8. From such familiar observations and reflections, children may be convinced, with absolute certainty, that there must be a being who has been the creator of all the things which they see. Now when you think that of all the substances about you, not one

can have been its own creator, and when you see the vast multitude of things, their variety, their size, their curious forms and structures, you will at once conclude that the Being who could make such things must possess immense power, altogether superior to the power of any being that you see on the earth. You will then be led to inquire who is this Being, and where is he.

9. Here not only children, but the wisest philosophers are brought to a stand. We are compelled to believe that there is a Being of vast and unlimited power, who has created whatever we see; but who he is or where he is, we cannot know by our own observation or reason. As we cannot see this Being, we cannot, by the help of reason, know anything of his manner of existence, or of his power, except what we learn from his works, or from revelation. If we had been left to gather all our knowledge of the creator from his works, our knowledge of him must have been very imperfect. But the creator has not left mankind in ignorance on this subject. He has graciously revealed his character to man; and his revelations are recorded in a book, which by way of eminence, is called the *Bible.*

10. From the Bible we learn that God is a *Spirit*; hence we cannot see him. Spirit is not visible to human eyes. Yet we need not wonder that a substance which is invisible should possess amazing power. We cannot see the air or wind; yet we know by observation, that this fine, subtil fluid is a substance that supports our life, and when in rapid motion, it has immense force. We conclude then that a Being, consisting of pure spirit, may possess all the power necessary to the formation of the sun, moon and stars, and every thing that we can see or feel. This great Being, in our language, is called *God.* He is a spirit that extends through the universe.

11. The scriptures inform us that God is not only all-powerful, but all-wise: and his wisdom is dis-

played in the admirable structure of whatever he has made; in the adaptation of every thing to its proper uses; in the exact order and beautiful arrangement and harmony of all parts of creation.

The scriptures inform us also that God is a benevolent Being. " God is love," and we have abundant evidence of this truth in the works of creation. God has not only made men and animals to inhabit the earth, but he has furnished the earth with every thing that is necessary for their support and welfare. The earth is stocked with plants, which are food for animals, of various kinds, as well as for man; and plants and animals furnish man with food and clothing and shelter from the inclemency of the weather. The sea and rivers and lakes are also stocked with animals that supply food and other conveniences for man. The earth contains inexhaustible stores for supplying the wants and desires of living creatures.

12. We learn also from the Bible that God is a holy Being; that is, he is perfectly free from any sinful attributes or dispositions. If God was a wicked or malevolent Being, he would have contrived and formed every thing on earth to make his creatures miserable. Instead of this, we know from observation as well as experience, he has made every thing for their comfort and happiness. Having learned from the scriptures and from the works of creation, the character of God, and that he is your creator; the next inquiry is, in what relation do you stand to your maker, and what is his will respecting your conduct.

13. The first and most important point to be decided in your minds is that God is your *Supreme or Sovereign Ruler.* On this point, there can be no room for doubt; for nothing can be more evident than that the Being who creates another, has a perfect, indisputable right to govern him. God has then a complete right to direct all the actions of the beings he has made. To the lower animals God has given

certain propensities, called instincts, which lead them to the means of their own subsistence and safety.

14. Man is a being of a higher order ; he is furnished with understanding or intellect, and with powers of reason, by which he is able to understand what God requires of him, and to judge of what is right and wrong. These faculties are the attributes of the *soul*, or spiritual part of man, which constitutes him a *moral* being, and exalts him to a rank in creation much superior to that of any other creature on earth.

15. Being satisfied that God is your creator and rightful governor, the next inquiry is, what is his will concerning you ; for what purpose did he make you and endow you with reason? A wise being would not have made you without a wise purpose. It is very certain then that God requires you to perform some duties, and fill some useful station among other beings.

16. The next inquiry then is, what you are to do and what you are to forbear, in order to act the part which your maker has assigned to you in the world. This you cannot know with certainty without the help of revelation. But here you are not left without the means of knowledge ; for God has revealed his will, and has given commands for the regulation of your conduct.

17. The Bible contains the commands of God ; that book is full of rules to direct your conduct on earth ; and from that book you may obtain all you want to know, respecting your relation to God, and to your fellow men, and respecting the duties which these relations require you to perform. Your duties are comprised in two classes ; one including such as are to be performed directly to God himself ; the other, those which are to be performed directly to your fellow men.

18. The first and great command is, to love the Lord your God with all the heart and soul and mind

and strength. This supreme love to God is the first, the great, the indispensable duty of every rational being. Without this no person can yield acceptable obedience to his maker. The reasonableness of this command is obvious. God is a Being of perfect excellence, and the only being of which we have any knowledge, who possesses this character. Goodness or holiness is the only source of real happiness; it is therefore necessary to be holy in order to be happy. As the character of God is the only perfect model of holiness, it follows that all God's creatures who are intended to be happy, must have the like character. But men will not aim to possess the character of holiness, unless they love it as the chief good. Hence the necessity of loving God with supreme affection.

19. Sin is the source of all evil. If sin was admitted into heaven, it would disturb the happiness of the celestial abode. Hence God has determined that no sinner shall be admitted into heaven. Before men can be received there, they must be purified from sin and sinful propensities. As this world is a state in which men are prepared for heaven, if prepared at all, it is indispensable that while they are in this world, they must be purified in heart, their evil affections must be subdued, and their prevailing dispositions must be holy. Thus when they are sanctified, and supreme love to God rules in their heart, they become qualified for the enjoyment of bliss with God and other holy beings.

20. It is true that, in this world, men do not become perfectly holy; but God has provided a Redeemer whose example on earth was a perfect model of holy obedience to God's law, which example men are to imitate as far as they are able; and God accepts the penitent sinner's cordial faith in Christ, accompanied with sincere repentance, and humble submission and obedience to his commands, in the place of perfect holiness of character.

21. The duties which you owe directly to God are

entire, unwavering faith in his promises, reverence of his character, and frequent prayer and worship. Unbelief is a great sin, and so is profaneness, irreverence, contempt of his character and laws, neglect of prayer and of worship, public and private. All worship of images, and saints is an abomination to God; it is idolatry which is strictly forbidden in the Bible; and all undue attachment to the pleasures, the amusements, and honors of the world, is a species of idolatry.

22. The second class of duties comprehends all such as you are bound to perform to your fellow men. These duties are very numerous, and require to be studied with care. The general law on this subject, is prescribed by Christ in these words, "Thou shalt love thy neighbor as thyself." You are bound to do that to others which you desire them to do to you. This law includes all the duties of respect to superiors, and of justice and kindness to all men.

23. It has already been stated to you, that you are to obey your parents; and although obedience to other superiors may not always be required of you, yet you are bound to yield them due honor and respect in all the concerns of life. Nothing can be more improper than a neglect or violation of this respect. It is a beautiful anecdote, recorded of the Spartan youth, that in a public meeting, young persons rose from their seats, when a venerable old man entered the assembly. It makes no difference whether the aged man is an acquaintance or a stranger; whoever he may be, always give him the precedence. In public places, and at public tables, it is extreme rudeness and ill manners, for the young to thrust themselves into the highest and best seats.

24. The law of kindness extends also to the treatment of equals. Civility requires that to them all persons should give a preference; and if they do not accept it, the offer always manifests good breeding. and wins affection. Never claim too much; modesty

will usually gain more than is demanded ; but arrogance will gain less. Modest, unassuming manners conciliate esteem; bold, obtrusive manners excite resentment or disgust.

25. As mankind are all one family, the rule of loving our neighbor as ourselves, extends to the performance of all duties of kindness to persons of all nations and all conditions of men. Persons of all nations, of all ranks, and conditions, high and low, rich and poor, and of all sects or denominations, are our brethren, and our *neighbors* in the sense which Christ intended to use the word in his precept. This comprehensive rule of duty cannot be limited by any acts of our own. Any private association of men for the purpose of contracting the rule, and confining our benevolence to such associations, is a violation of the divine commands. Christ healed the sick, and the lame, without any regard to the nation or sect to which they belonged.

26. One of the most important rules of social conduct is *justice*. This consists positively in rendering to every person what is due to him and negatively, in avoiding every thing that may impair his rights. Justice embraces the rights of property, the rights of personal liberty and safety, and the rights of character.

27. In regard to property, you are to pay punctually all your just debts. When a debt becomes payable to another, you cannot withhold or delay payment without a violation of his right. By failure or delay of payment, you keep that which belongs to another. But the rule of justice extends to every act which can affect the property of another. If you borrow any article of your neighbor, you are to use it with care and not injure the value of it. If you borrow a book or any utensil, and injure it, you take a portion of your neighbor's property. Yet heedless people who would not steal twenty five cents from another, often think nothing of injuring a borrowed utensil, to twice or five times that amount.

28. In like manner, one who takes a lease of a house or land, is bound to use it in such a manner as to injure it as little as possible. Yet how often do the lessees of real estate, strive to gain as much as possible from the use of it, while they suffer the bildings and fences to go to ruin, to the great injury of the owner! This is one of the most common species of immorality. But all needless waste and all diminution of the value of property in the hands of a lessee, proceeding from negligence, amounts to the same thing as the taking of so much of the owner's property without right. It is not considered as stealing, but it is a species of fraud that is as really immoral as stealing.

29. The command of God," Thou shalt not steal," is very comprehensive, extending to the prohibition of every species of fraud. Stealing is the taking of something from the possession of another clandestinely for one's own use. This may be done by entering the house of another at night, and taking his property; or by taking goods from a shop secretly or by entering upon another's land and taking his horse or his sheep. These customary modes of stealing are punishable by law.

30. But, there are many other ways of taking other men's property secretly, which are not so liable to be detected. If a stone is put into a bag of cotton intended for a distant market, it increases the weight, and the purchaser of that bag who pays for it at its weight, buys a stone in stead of its weight in cotton. In this case, the man who first sells the bag knowing it to contain a stone, takes from the purchaser by fraud as much money as the weight of the stone produces, that is, as much as the same weight of cotton is worth. This is as criminal as it would be to enter his house and steal so much money.

31. If butter or lard is put up for a foreign or distant market, it should be put up in a good state, and the real quality should be such as it *appears* to be.

If any deception is practiced, by covering that which is bad by that which is good or by other means, all the price of the article which it brings beyond the real worth, is so much money taken from the purchaser by fraud, which falls within the criminality of stealing. If a buyer of the article in Europe or the West Indies is thus defrauded, *he* may never be able to know who has done the wrong; but God knows and will punish the wrong doer. It is as immoral to cheat a foreigner as to cheat a neighbor.

32. Not only property in money and goods is to be respected; but the property in fruit growing in orchards and gardens. A man's apples, pears, peaches, and melons are as entirely his own, as his goods or his coin. Every person who climbs over a fence or enters by a gate into another's inclosure without permission is a trespasser; and if he takes fruit secretly, he is a thief. It makes no difference that a pear or an apple or a melon is of small value; a man has as exclusive a right to a *cent* or a *melon* as he has to a *dollar*, a *dime* or an *eagle*.

33. If in a country where apples are abundant, men do not notice the taking of a few apples to eat, yet this indulgence is not to be considered as giving a right to take them. Where the injury is trifling, men in neighborhoods may do such things by consent. But there are many species of fruit so rare as to be cultivated with much labor and protected with care. Such fruit is often valued even more than money. The stealing of such fruit is one of the most common crimes, and as disgraceful to a civilized and christian people as it is common. Let every man or boy who enters another's inclosure and steals fruit be assured he is as guilty as one who enters another's house and takes the same value in money.

34. If in making payment or counting money, a mistake occurs by which a sum falls into your hands, which belongs to another person, you are as much bound by moral duty to correct the mistake and re-

store the money to the rightful owner, as you would be *not* to take it by theft. If persons suppose that because this money falls into their hands by mistake, and the mistake may never be known to the person who has a right to the money; this makes no difference in the point of morality; the concealment of the mistake and the keeping of the money are dishonest, and fall within the command "Thou shalt not steal."

35. When a man is hired to work for another by the day, the week or the month, he is bound to perform what he undertakes; and if no particular amount of labor is promised, he is bound to do the work which is ordinarily done in such cases. If a man hired to do a day's work spends half the day in idleness, he defrauds his employer of a part of his due; that is of one half the value of a day's labor. If the price of labor is one dollar for the day, then to waste half the day in idleness is to defraud the employer of half a dollar; this is as dishonest as to take half a dollar from his chest.

36. When a mechanic contracts to build a house or a ship, he is bound to perform the work in the manner which is promised. If he performs the work slightly, and with workmanship inferior to that which is promised and understood at the time of contracting, he defrauds his employer. Neglect of duty, in such a case, is as essentially immoral as the positive act of taking property from another without his consent.

37. The adulteration of liquors and drugs is extremely criminal. By adulteration, the value of a thing is diminished; and if an adulterated liquor or drug is sold for that which is genuine, a fraud is committed on the purchaser. The adulteration of wines is one of the most common and flagrant immoralities in commercial countries. The adulteration of drugs may be even more iniquitous, for then the physician cannot rely on their effects in healing the sick. All

classes of people, but especially the common people, are continually subjected to frauds by such adulterations. A glass of genuine unadulterated wine is scarcely to be found, and foul mixtures are often used as medicines, for no pure wine is to be had in the neighborhood.

33. The modes used to defraud men in the kind or in the quantity or quality of commodities offered for sale, are almost innumerable. They extend to almost every thing in which fraud is not easily detected. This is a melancholy picture of the state of society; exhibiting unequivocal evidence of the depravity of men. It shows that the love of money is the root of all evil—a principle so powerful in the human heart as to overcome all regard to truth, morality and reputation.

39. In all your dealings with men, let a strict regard to veracity and justice govern all your actions. Uprightness in dealings secures confidence and the confidence of our fellow men is the basis of reputation, and often a source of prosperity. Men are always ready to assist those whom they can trust; and a good character in men of business often raises them to wealth and distinction. On the other hand hypocrisy, trickishness, and want of punctuality and of fairness in trade often sink men into meanness and poverty. Hence we see that the divine commands, which require men to be just, are adapted to advance their temporal as well as their spiritual interest.

40. Not only are theft and fraud of all kinds forbidden by the laws of God and man, but all kinds of injury or annoyance of the peace, security, rights and prosperity of men. The practice of boys and of men, who do mischief for sport, is as wrong in morality as it is degrading to the character. To pull down or deface a sign-board; to break or deface a mile-stone; to cut and disfigure benches or tables, in a school house, court house or church; to place obstacles in the highway; to pull down or injure fences; to tar-

nish the walls of houses or the boards of a fence, and similar tricks that injure property or disturb the peace of society, are not only mean but immoral. Why will rational beings indulge in such feats of mischief and folly? Men are not made to injure and annoy one another; but to assist them : not to do harm, but to do good; not to lessen but to increase the prosperity and enjoyments of their fellow men.

41. But you are required to be just not only to the property, but to the reputation of others. A man's reputation is dearer to him than his property, and he that detracts from the good name of another is as criminal as the thief who takes his property. Say nothing of your neighbor maliciously, nor spread reports about him to lessen his reputation. On the other hand vindicate his conduct in all cases when you can do it with a clear conscience. If you cannot defend it, remain silent.

42. Nor are you to be less careful of the rights of others, than of their reputation, and property. By the laws of creation, and by our civil constitution, all men have equal rights to protection, to liberty, and to the free enjoyment of all the benefits and privileges of government. All secret attempts, by associations or otherwise to give to one set of men or one party, advantages over another, are mean, dishonorable and immoral. All secret combinations of men to gain for themselves or their party, advantages in preferments to office, are trepasses upon the rights of others.

43. In every condition of life, and in forming your opinions on every subject, let it be an established principle in regulating your conduct, that nothing can be *honorable* which is *morally wrong*. Men who disregard or disbelieve revelation often err from the true standard of honor, by substituting public opinion or false maxims for the divine laws. The character of God, his holy attributes, and perfect law constitute the only models and rules of excellence and true honor. Whatever deviates from these models

and rules must be wrong, and dishonorable. Crime and vice are therefore not only repugnant to duty, and to human happiness; but are always derogatory to reputation. All vice implies defect and meanness in human character.

44. In whatever laudable occupation you are destined to labor, be steady in an industrious application of time. Time is given to you for employment, not for waste. Most men are obliged to labor for subsistence; and this is a happy arrangement of things by divine appointment; as labor is one of the best preservatives both of health and of moral habits. But if you are not under the necessity of laboring for subsistence, let your time be occupied in something which shall do good to yourselves and your fellow men. Idleness tends to lend men into vicious pleasures: and to waste time is to abuse the gifts of God.

45. With most persons, the gaining of property is a primary object, and one which demands wisdom in planning business, and assiduous care, attention and industry in conducting it. But it is perhaps more difficult to keep property than to gain it; as men while acquiring property are more economical and make more careful calculations of profit and loss, than when they hold large possessions. Men who inherit large possessions are particularly liable to waste their property, and fall into poverty. The greatest hereditary estates in this country are usually dissipated by the second or third generation. The sons and grandsons of the richest men are often hewers of wood and drawers of water to the sons and grandsons of their father's and grandfather's servants.

46. As a general rule in the expenditure of money, it is safest to earn money before you spend it, and to spend every year less than you earn. By this means, you will secure a comfortable subsistence, and be enabled to establish your children in some honest calling; at the same time, this practice will furnish the means of contributing to the wants of the poor, and

to the promotion of institutions for civilizing and christianizing heathen nations. This is a great and indispensable duty.

47. In your mode of living, be not ambitious of adopting every extravagant fashion. Many fashions are not only inconvenient and expensive, but inconsistent with good taste. The love of finery is of savage origin; the rude inhabitant of the forest delights to deck his person with pieces of shining metal, with painted fethers, and with some appendage dangling from the ears or nose. The same love of finery infects civilized men and women, more or less in every country, and the body is adorned with brilliant gems and gaudy attire. But true taste demands great simplicity of dress. A well made person is one of the most beautiful of all God's works, and a simple, neat dress displays this person to the best advantage.

48. In all sensual indulgences be temperate. God has given to men all good things for use and enjoyment; but enjoyment consists in using food and drink only for the nourishment and sustenance of the body, and all amusements and indulgences should be in moderation. Excess never affords enjoyment; but always brings inconvenience, pain or disease. In selecting food and drink, take such as best support the healthy functions of the body, avoid as much as possible, the stimulus of high-seasoned food; and reject the use of ardent spirits, as the most injurious and most fatal poison.

49. When you become entitled to exercise the right of voting for public officers, let it be impressed on your mind that God commands you to choose for rulers, *just men who will rule in the fear of God.* The preservation of a republican government depends on the faithful discharge of this duty; if the citizens neglect their duty and place unprincipled men in office, the government will soon be corrupted; laws will be made, not for the public good, so much as for selfish or local purpo ses; corrupt or in-

competent men will be appointed to execute the laws; the public revenues will be squandered on unworthy men; and the rights of the citizens will be violated or disregarded. If a republican government fails to secure public prosperity and happiness, it must be because the citizens neglect the divine commands, and elect bad men to make and administer the laws. Intriguing men can never be safely trusted.

50. To young men I would recommend that their treatment of females should be always characterized by kindness, delicacy and respect.   The tender sex look to men for protection and support. Females when properly educated and devoted to their appropriate duties, are qualified to add greatly to the happiness of society, and of domestic life. Endowed with finer sensibilities than men, they are quick to learn and to practice the civilities and courtesies of life; their reputation requires the nice observance of the rules of decorum; and their presence and example impose most salutary restraints on the ruder passions and less polished manners of the other sex.   In the circle of domestic duties, they are cheerful companions of their husbands; they give grace and joy to prosperity; consolation and support to adversity. When we see an affectionate wife devoted to her do mestic duties, cheering her husband with smiles, and as a mother, carefully tending and anxiously guard ing her children and forming their minds to virtue and to piety; or watching with conjugal or maternal tenderness over the bed of sickness: we cannot fail to number among the chief temporal advantages of christianity, the elevation of the female character. Let justice then be done to their merits; guard their purity; defend their honor; treat them with tenderness and respect.

51. For a knowledge of the human heart, and the characters of men, it is customary to resort to the writings of Shakspeare, and of other dramatic authors, and to biography, novels, tales and fictitious narra-

tives. But whatever amusement may be derived from such writings, they are not the best authorities for a knowledge of mankind. The most perfect maxims and examples for regulating your social conduct and domestic economy, as well as the best rules of morality and religion, are to be found in the Bible. The history of the Jews presents the true character of man in all its forms. All the traits of human character, good and bad; all the passions of the human heart; all the principles which guide and misguide men in society, are depicted in that short history, with an artless simplicity that has no parallel in modern writings. As to maxims of wisdom or prudence, the Proverbs of Solomon furnish a complete system, and sufficient, if carefully observed, to make any man wise, prosperous and happy. The observation, that "a soft answer turneth away wrath," if strictly observed by men, would prevent half the broils and contentions that inflict wretchedness on society and families.

52. Let your first care, through life, be directed to support and extend the influence of the christian religion, and the observance of the sabbath. This is the only system of religion which has ever been offered to the consideration and acceptance of men, which has even probable evidence of a divine original; It is the only religion that honors the character and moral government of the Supreme Being: it is the only religion which gives even a probable account of the origin of the world, and of the dispensations of God towards mankind; it is the only religion which teaches the character and laws of God, with our relations and our duties to him: it is the only religion which assures us of an immortal existence; which offer the means of everlasting salvation, and consoles mankind under the inevitable calamities of the present life.

53. But were we assured that there is to be no future life, and that men are to perish at death like

the beasts of the field; the moral principles and pre-cepts contained in the scriptures ought to form the basis of all our civil constitutions and laws. These principles and precepts have truth, immutable truth, for their foundation; and they are adapted to the wants of men in every condition of life. They are the best principles and precepts, because they are exactly adapted to secure the practice of universal justice and kindness among men; and of course to prevent crimes, war and disorders in society. No human laws dictated by different principles from those in the gospel, can ever secure these objects. All the miseries and evils which men suffer from vice, crime, ambition, injustice, oppression, slavery and war, proceed from their despising or neglecting the precepts contained in the Bible.

54. As the means of temporal happiness, then, the christian religion ought to be received, and maintained with firm and cordial support. It is the real source of all genuine republican principles. It teaches the equality of men as to rights and duties; and while it forbids all oppression, it commands due subordination to law and rulers. It requires the young to yield obedience to their parents, and enjoins upon men the duty of selecting their rulers from their fellow citizens of mature age, sound wisdom and real religion—" men who fear God and hate covetousness." The ecclesiastical establishments of Europe which serve to support tyrannical governments, are not the christian religion, but abuses and corruptions of it. The religion of Christ and his apostles, in its primitive simplicity and purity, unencumbered with the trappings of power and the pomp of ceremonies, is the surest basis of a republican government.

55. Never cease then to give to religion, to its institutions and to its ministers your strenuous support. The clergy in this country are not possessed of rank and wealth; they depend for their influence on their talents and learning, on their private vir-

tues and public services. They are the firm support-
ers of law and good order, the friends of peace, the
expounders and teachers of christian doctrines, the
instructors of youth, the promoters of benevolence,
of charity, and of all useful improvements. During
the war of the revolution, the clergy were generally
friendly to the cause of the country. The present
generation can hardly have a tolerable idea of the
influence of the New England clergy, in sustaining
the patriotic exertions of the people,under the appal-
ling discouragements of the war. The writer remem-
bers their good offices with gratitude. Those men
therefore who attempt to impair the influence of that
respectable order, in this country, attempt to under-
mine the best supports of religion ; and those who destroy the influence and authority of the christian religion, sap the foundations of public order, of liberty
and of republican government.

56. For instruction then in social, religious and
civil duties resort to the scriptures for the best precepts and most excellent examples for imitation. The
example of unhesitating faith and obedience in Abraham, when he promptly prepared to offer his son
Isaac, as a burnt offering, at the command of God,
is a perfect model of that trust in God which becomes
dependent beings. The history of Joseph furnishes
one of the most charming examples of fraternal affection and of filial duty and respect for a venerable father, ever exhibited in human life. Christ and his
apostles presented, in their lives, the most perfect example of disinterested benevolence, unaffected kindness, humility, patience in adversity, forgiveness of
injuries, love to God and to all mankind. If men
would universally cultivate these religious affections
and virtuous dispositions, with as much diligence as
they cultivate human science, and refinement of manners, the world would soon become a terrestrial par-
adise.

THE

AMERICAN

SPELLING BOOK;

CONTAINING

THE RUDIMENTS

OF THE

ENGLISH LANGUAGE,

FOR THE

USE OF SCHOOLS

IN THE

UNITED STATES.

BY NOAH WEBSTER, ESQ.

A MORAL CATECHISM.

Question. What is moral virtue?

Answer. It is an honest upright conduct in all our dealings with men.

Q. What rules have we to direct us in our moral conduct?

A. God's word, contained in the bible, has furnished all necessary rules to direct our conduct.

Q. In what part of the bible are these rules to be found?

A. In almost every part; but the most important duties between men are summed up in the beginning of Matthew, in Christ's Sermon on the Mount.

An Easy Standard of Pronunciation.

Of HUMILITY.

Q. What is humility ?
A. A lowly temper of mind
Q. What are the advantages of humility?
A. The advantages of humility in this life are very numerous and great. The humble man has few or no ene mies. Every one loves him and is ready to do him good. If he is rich and prosperous, people do not envy him : if he is poor and unfortunate, every one pities him and is disposed to alleviate his distresses.
Q. What is pride?
A. A lofty high minded disposition.
Q. Is pride commendable?
A. By no means. A modest self-approving opinion of our own good deeds is very right. -It is natural—it is a-greeable, and a spur to good actions. But we should not suffer our hearts to be blown up with pride, whatever great and good deeds we have done; for pride brings upon us the ill-will of mankind, and the displeasure of our Maker.
Q. What effect has humility upon our own minds?
A. Humility is attended with peace of mind and self-satisfaction. The humble man is not disturbed with cross accidents, and is never fretful and uneasy ; nor does he repine when others grow rich. He is contented, because his mind is at ease.
Q What is the effect of pride on a man's happiness ?
A. Pride exposes a man to numberless disappointments and mortifications. The proud man expects more attention and respect will be paid to him, than he deserves, or than others are willing to pay him. He is neglected, laughed at and despised, and this treatment frets him, so that his own mind becomes a seat of torment. A proud man cannot be a happy man.
Q. What has Christ said, respecting the virtue of humility ?
A. He has said, " Blessed are the poor in spirit ; for theirs is the kingdom of heaven." Poorness of spirit, is humility ; and this humble temper prepares a man for heaven, where all is peace and love.

An Easy Standard of Pronunciation.

Of MERCY.

Q. *What is mercy?*

A. It is tenderness of heart.

Q. *What are the advantages of this virtue?*

A. The exercise of it tends to diffuse happiness and lessen the evils of life. Rulers of a merciful temper will make their *good* subjects happy ; and will not torment the *bad*, with needless severity. Parents and masters will not abuse their children and servants with harsh treatment. More love, more confidence, more happiness, will subsist among men, and of course society will be happier.

Q. *Should not beasts as well as men be treated with mercy?*

A. They ought indeed. It is wrong to give needless pain even to a beast. Cruelty to the brutes shows a man has a hard heart, and if a man is unfeeling to a beast, he will not have much feeling for men. If a man treats his beast with cruelty, beware of trusting yourself in his power. He will probably make a severe master and a cruel husband.

Q. *How does cruelty show its effects?*

A. A cruel disposition is usually exercised upon those who are under its power. Cruel rulers make severe laws which injure the persons and properties of their subjects. Cruel officers execute laws in a severe manner, when it is not necessary for public good. A cruel husband abuses his wife and children. A cruel master acts the tyrant over his apprentices and servants. The effects of cruelty are, hatred, quarrels, tumults and wretchedness.

Q. *What does Christ say of the merciful man?*

A. He says he is "blessed, for he shall obtain mercy." He who shows mercy and tenderness to others, will be treated with tenderness and compassion himself.

Of PEACE-MAKERS.

Q. *Who are peace-makers?*

A. All who endeavor to prevent quarrels and disputes among men ; or to reconcile those who are separated by strife.

Q. *Is it unlawful to contend with others on any occasion?*

A. It is impossible to avoid some differences with

An Easy Standard of Pronunciation.

men ; but disputes should be always conducted with temper and moderation. The man who keeps his temper
will not be rash, and do or say things which he will after-
wards repent of. And though men should sometimes dif-
fer, still they should be friends. They should be ready
to do kind offices to each other.

Q. *What is the reward of the peace-maker?*

A. He shall be " blessed, and called the child of God."
The mild, peaceable, friendly man, resembles God. What
an amiable character is this ! To be like our heavenly
Father, that lovely, perfect and glorious being who is the
source of all good, is to be the best and happiest of men.

Of PURITY of HEART.

Q. *What is a pure heart?*

A. A heart free from all bad desires, and inclined to
conform to the divine will in all things.

Q. *Should a man's intentions as well as his actions be
good?*

A. Most certainly. Actions cannot be called *good,* unless they proceed from good motives. We should wish
to see and make all men better and happier—we should
rejoice at their prosperity. This is benevolence.

Q. *What reward is promised to the pure in heart.*

A. Christ has declared " they shall see God." A pure
heart is like God, and those who possess it shall dwell in
his presence and enjoy his favor for ever.

Of ANGER.

Q. *Is it right ever to be angry?*

A. It is right in certain cases that we should be angry ; as when gross affronts are offered to us, and injuries done us by design. A suitable spirit of resentment,
in such cases, will obtain justice for us, and protect us
from further insults.

Q. *By what rule should anger be governed?*

A. We should never be angry without cause ; that is,
we should be certain that a person *means* to affront, injure or insult us, before we suffer ourselves to be angry.
It is wrong, it is mean, it is a mark of a little mind to
take fire at every little trifling dispute. And when we
have real cause to be angry, we should observe mode-

An Easy Standard of Pronunciation.

ration. We should never be in a passion. A passionate man is like a mad man, and is always inexcusable. We should be cool even in anger ; and be angry no longer than to obtain justice. In short, we should " be angry and sin not."

Of REVENGE.

Q. *What is revenge ?*

A. It is to injure a man because he has injured us.

Q. *Is this justifiable ?*

A. Never, in any possible case. Revenge is perhaps the meanest, as well as wickedest vice in society.

Q. *What shall a man do to obtain justice when he is in-ured ?*

A. In general, laws have made provision for doing justice to every man; and it is right and honorable, when a man is injured, that he should seek a recompence. But a recompence is all he can demand, and of that he should not be his own judge, but should submit the matter to judges appointed by authority.

Q. *But suppose a man insults us in such a manner that the law cannot give us redress ?*

A. Then forgive him. " If a man strikes you on one cheek, turn the other to him," and let him repeat the abuse, rather than strike him.

Q. *But if we are in danger from the blows of another, may we not defend ourselves?*

A. Most certainly. We have always a right to defend our persons, property and families. But we have no right to fight and abuse people merely for revenge. It is nobler to forgive. " Love your enemies—bless them that curse you—do good to them that hate you—pray for them that use you ill."—these are the commands of the blessed Savior of men. The man who does this is great and good ; he is as much above the little, mean, revengeful man, as virtue is above vice, or as heaven is higher than hell.

Of JUSTICE

Q. *What is justice ?*

A. It is giving to every man his due.

Q. *Is it awlays easy to know what is just ?*

A. It is generally easy ; and where there is any diffi-

An Easy Standard of Pronunciation.

culty in determining, let a man consult the golden rule —" To do to others, what he could reasonably wish they should do to him, in the same circumstances."

Q. What are the ill effects of injustice ?

A. If a man does injustice, or rather, if he refuses to do justice, he must be compelled. Then follows a law suit, with a series of expenses, and what is worse, ill-blood and enmity between the parties. Somebody is always the worse for law-suits, and of course society is less happy.

Of GENEROSITY.

Q. What is generosity ?

A. It is some act of kindness performed for another which strict justice does not demand.

Q. Is this a virtue ?

A. It is indeed a noble virtue. To do justice, is well ; but to do more than justice, is still better, and may proceed from nobler motives.

Q. What has Christ said respecting generosity ?

A. He has commanded us to be generous in this passage, " Whosoever shall compel (or urge) you to go a *mile*, go with him *two.*

Q. Are we to perform this literally ?

A. The meaning of the command will not always require this.—But in general we are to do more for others than they ask, provided we can do it, without essentially injuring ourselves. We ought cheerfully to suffer many inconveniences to oblige others, though we are not required to do ourselves any essential injury.

Q. Of what advantage is generosity to the man who exercises it ?

A. It lays others under obligations to the generous man ; and the probability is that he will be repaid three fold. Every man on earth wants favors at some time or other in his life ; and if we will not help others, others will not help us. It is for a man's interest to be generous.

Q. Ought we do kind actions, because it is for our interest ?

A. This may be a motive at all times ; but if it is the principal motive, it is less honorable. We ought to do

An Easy Standard of Pronunciation.

good, as we have opportunity, at all times and to all men, whether we expect a reward or not; for if we do good, somebody is the happier for it. This alone is reason enough, why we should do all the good in our power.

Of GRATITUDE.

Q. What is gratitude ?

A. A thankfulness of heart for favors received.

Q. Is it a duty to be thankful for favors ?

A. It is a duty and a virtue. A man who does not feel grateful for kind acts done for him by others, does not deserve favors of any kind. He ought to be shut out from the society of the good. He is worse than a savage, for a savage never forgets an act of kindness.

Q. What is the effect of true kindness ?

A. It softens the heart towards the generous man, and every thing which subdues the pride and other unsocial passions of the heart, fits a man to be a better citizen, a better neighbor, a better husband and a better friend. A man who is sensible of favors and ready to acknowledge them is more inclined to perform kind offices, not only towards his benefactor, but towards all others.

Of TRUTH.

Q. What is truth ?

A. It is speaking and acting agreeable to fact.

Q. Is it a duty to speak truth at all times ?

A. If we speak at all, we should tell the truth. It is not always necessary to tell what we know. There are many things which concern ourselves and others, which we had better not publish to the world.

Q. What rules are there respecting the publishing of truth ?

A. 1. When we are called upon to testify in courts, we should speak the whole truth and that without disguise. To leave out small circumstances, or to give a coloring to others, with a view to favor one side more than the other, is to the highest degree criminal.

2. When we know something of our neighbor which

An Easy Standard of Pronunciation.

is against his character, we may not publish it, unless
to prevent his doing an injury to another person.

3. When we sell any thing to another, we ought not
to represent the article to be better than it really is. If
there are faults in it which may easily be seen, the law
of man does not require us to inform the buyer of these
faults, because he may see them himself. But it is not
honorable nor generous, nor strictly honest to conceal
even apparent faults. But when faults are out of sight,
the seller ought to tell the buyer of them. If he does
not, he is a cheat and a downright knave.

Q. What are the ill effects of lying and deceiving ?

A. The man who lies, deceives or cheats, loses his reputation. No person will believe him, even when he
speaks the truth ; he is shunned as a pest to society.

Falsehood and cheating destroy all confidence between
man and man ; they raise jealousies and suspicions a-
mong men ; they thus weaken the bands of society and
destroy happiness. Besides, cheating often strips people
of their property and makes them poor and wretched.

Of CHARITY and GIVING ALMS.

What is charity ?

A. It signifies giving to the poor, or it is a favorable
opinion of men and their actions.

Q. When and how far is it our duty to give to the poor ?

A. When others really want what we can spare without material injury to ourselves, it is our duty to give
them something to relieve their wants.

*Q. When persons are reduced to want by their own la-
ziness and vices, by drunkenness, gambling and the like, is
it a duty to relieve them ?*

A. In general, it is not. The man who gives money
and provisions to a lazy, vicious man, becomes a par-
taker of his guilt. Perhaps it may be right, to give
such a man a meal of victuals to keep him from starv-
ing, and it is certainly right to feed his wife and family,
and make them comfortable.

Q. Who are the proper objects of charity ?

An Easy Standard of Pronunciation.

A. Persons who are reduced to want by sickness, un-
avoidable losses by fire, storms at sea or land, drouth or
accidents of other kinds.   To such persons we are commanded to give ; and it is our own interest to be chari-
table ; for we are all liable to misfortunes and may want
charity ourselves.

Q. In what manner should we bestow favors ?

A. We should do it with gentleness and affection ;
putting on no airs of pride and arrogance.   We should
also take no pains to publish our charities, but rather
conceal them ; for if we boast of our generosity, we
discover that we give from mean selfish motives.   Christ
commands us, in giving alms, not to let our left hand
know what our right hand doeth.

*Q. How can charity be exercised in our opinions of
others ?*

A. By thinking favorably of them and their actions.
Every man has his faults ; but charity will not put a
harsh construction on another's conduct.   It will not
charge his conduct to bad views and motives, unless this
appears very clear indeed.

OF AVARICE.

Q. What is avarice ?

A. An excessive desire of possessing wealth.

Q. Is this commendable ?

A. It is not ; but one of the meanest of vices.

Q. Can an avaricious man be an honest man ?

A. It is hardly possible ; for the lust of gain is almost
always accompanied with a disposition to take mean and
undue advantages of others.

Q. What effect has avarice upon the heart ?

A. It contracts the heart—narrows the sphere of benevolence—blunts all the fine feelings of sensibility, and
sours the mind towards society.   An avaricious man, a
miser, a niggard, is wrapped up in selfishness, like some
worms, which crawl about and eat for some time to fill
themselves, then wind themselves up in separate cover-
ings and die.

An Easy Standard of Pronunciation.

Q. What injury is done by avarice to society.

A. Avarice gathers together more property, than the owner wants, and keeps it hoarded up, where it does no good. The poor are thus deprived of some business—some means of support; the property gains nothing to the community; and somebody is less happy by means of this hoarding of wealth.

Q. In what proportion does avarice do hurt?

A. In an exact proportion to its power of doing good: The miser's *heart* grows *less*, in proportion as his *estate* grows *larger*. The more money he has, the more he has people in his power, and the more he grinds the face of the poor. The larger the tree and the more spreading the branches, the more small plants are shaded and robbed of their nourishment.

Of FRUGALITY and ECONOMY.

Q. What is the distinction between frugality and avarice?

A. Frugality is a prudent saving of property from needless waste. Avarice gathers more and spends less than is necessary

Q. What is economy?

A. It is frugality in expenses—it is a prudent management of one's estate. It disposes of property for useful purposes without waste.

Q. How far does true economy extend?

A. To the saving of every thing which it is not necessary to spend for comfort and convenience; and the keeping one's expenses within his income or earnings.

Q. What is wastefulness?

A. It is the spending of money for what is not wanted. If a man drinks a dram which is not necessary for him, or buys a cane which he does not want, he wastes his money. He injures *himself*, as much as if he had thrown away his money.

Q. Is not waste often occasioned by mere negligence?

A. Very often. The man who does not keep his house and barn well covered; who does not keep good fences about his fields; who suffers his farming uten-

An Easy Standard of Pronunciation.

sils to lie out in the rain or on the ground ; or his cattle
to waste manure in the high way, is as much a spend-
thrift as the tavern haunter, the tipler and the gamester.

Q. *Do not careless, slovenly people work harder than the
neat and orderly ?*

A. Much harder. It is more labor to destroy a growth
of sturdy weeds, than to pull them up when they first
spring from the ground. So the disorders and abuses
which grow out of a sloven's carelessness, in time, become almost incurable. Hence such people work like
slaves and to little effect.

Of INDUSTRY.

Q. *What is industry ?*

A. It is a diligent attention to business in our several
occupations.

Q. *Is labor a curse or a blessing ?*

A. Hard labor or drudgery is often a curse, by making life toilsome and painful. But constant moderate
labor is the greatest of blessings.

Q. *Why then do people complain of it ?*

A. Because they do not know the evils of *not* laboring.
Labor keeps the body in health and makes men relish
all their enjoyments. " The sleep of the laboring man
is sweet," so is his food. He walks cheerful and whist-
ling about his field or his shop, and scarcely knows pain.

The rich and indolent first lose their health for want
of action—They turn pale, their bodies are enfeebled,
they lose their appetite for food and sleep, they yawn
out a tasteless life of dullness, without pleasure, and often
useless to the world.

Q. *What are the other good effects of industry ?*

A. One effect is to procure an estate. Our Creator
has kindly united our duty, our interest and happiness ;
for the same labor which makes us healthy and cheerful, gives us wealth.

Another good effect of industry is, to keep men from
vice. Not all the moral discourses ever delivered to
mankind, have so much effect in checking the bad passions of men, in keeping order and peace, and maintaining

An Easy Standard of Pronunciation.

moral virtue in society, as *industry.* *Business* is a source of health, of prosperity, of virtue and obedience to law.

To make good subjects and good citizens, the first requisite is to educate every young person, in some kind of business. The possession of millions should not excuse a young man from application to business ; and that parent or guardian who suffers his child or his ward to be bred in idleness, becomes accessary to the vices and disorders of society.—He is guilty of " not providing for his household, and is worse than an infidel."

Of CHEERFULNESS.

Q. Is cheerfulness a virtue ?

A. It doubtless is. and a moral duty to practice it.

Q. Can we be cheerful when we please ?

A. In general it depends much on ourselves. We can often mold our tempers into a cheerful frame — We can frequent company and other objects calculated to inspire us with cheerfulness. To indulge an habitual gloominess of mind is weakness and sin.

Q. What are the effects of cheerfulness on ourselves ?

A. Cheerfulness is a great preservative of health, over which it is our duty to watch with care. We have no right to sacrifice our health by the indulgence of a gloomy state of mind. Besides a cheerful man, will do more business, and do it better, than a melancholy one.

Q. What are the effects of cheerfulness on others ?

A. Cheerfulness is readily communicated to others, by which means their happiness is increased. We are all influenced by sympathy, and naturally partake of the joys and sorrows of others.

Q. What effect has melancholy on the heart ?

A. It hardens and benums it.—It chills the warm affections of love and friendship, and prevents the exercise of the social passions. A melancholy person's life is all night and winter. It is as unnatural as perpetual darkness and frost.

Q. What shall one do, when overwhelmed with grief ?

A. The best method of expelling grief from the mind,

An Easy Standard of Pronunciation.

or of quieting its pains, is to change the objects that are about us ; to ride from place to place, and frequent cheerful company. It is our duty so to do, especially when grief sits heavy on the heart.

Q Is it not right to grieve for the loss of our friends ?

A. It is certainly right ; but we should endeavor to moderate our grief, and not suffer it to impair our health, or to grow into a settled melancholy. The use of grief is to soften the heart and make us better. But when our friends are dead, we can render them no further service: Our duty to them ends, when we commit them to the grave ; but our duty to ourselves, our families and surviving friends, requires that we perform to them the customary offices of life. We should therefore remember our departed friends only to imitate their virtues ; and not pine away with useless sorrow.

Q. Has not religion a tendency, to fill the mind with gloom ?

A. True religion never has this effect. Superstition and false notions of God, often make men gloomy ; but true rational piety and religion have the contrary effect. They fill the mind with joy and cheerfulness ; and the countenance of a truly pious man should always wear a serene smile.

Q. What has Christ said concerning gloomy Christians ?

A. He has pronounced them hypocrites ; and commanded his followers not to copy their sad countenances and disfigured faces ; but even in their acts of humiliation to " anoint their heads and wash their feet." Christ intended by this, that religion does not consist in, nor require a monkish sadness and gravity ; on the other hand he intimates, that such *appearances* of sanctity are generally the marks of hypocrisy. He expressly enjoins upon his followers, marks of cheerfulness. Indeed, the onlytrue ground of perpetual cheerfulness, is, a consciousness of ever having done well, and an assurance of divine favor.

FINIS.

NOTES

NOTES

NOTES

NOTES

NOTES

NOTES

NOTES

NOTES

NOTES

NOTES

ALSO AVAILABLE FROM WALLBUILDERS

Please go to **www.wallbuilders.com** to view our
numerous books, DVDs, CDs, and other resources
that will help you rediscover the true history of
America's moral, religious, and constitutional heritage.

You may also enjoy browsing through the
Historic Documents and Historic Writings section
in the "Library" at **www.wallbuilders.com**
to see the Founders own writings!

800-873-2845   ●   WWW.WALLBUILDERS.COM